I0616295

Faith to Flourish

By Veronica A. Burnett

Table of Contents

Dear Reader,

Allow me to share with you why I wrote this book. I wrote this book, not as an expert on faith. I believe we can all cultivate our faith. However, I wrote this book because I'm an expert on what it looks like to want to have faith but sometimes my analytical mind gets in the way. Sometimes my fear takes over. My over-thinking and rationalizing take over and faith goes out the window.

You see, I know what it's like to be the person who has had to have control over every aspect of her life. Stubborn to the fact that help is available because 'I should be able to handle everything on my own…I'm grown.' I know what it's like to want to do something big or different, not know the strategy and still press on with my limited knowledge, never once consulting God because, 'I got this.'

I know what it's like to talk about faith and trust, but not have it. I was also the one who could quote and read and study scriptures and encourage others to have faith but not have enough to believe for my own life to turn around. Let's not talk about how I prayed for others' miracles, breakthroughs and deliverance. I watched it happen. I watched God bless my friends in areas that I prayed for, yet, I didn't have that kind of faith in my prayers for myself.

How about this? I have seen beautiful love relationships for others, yet, I didn't believe it was possible for me too. So, I settled for less than God's best. I prayed and I cried, but didn't believe He could do the same thing for me.

Maybe you're like me or have experienced some of what I have and you are ready to begin growing in your faith. I will say this, being ready requires a few things: you must acknowledge that you want this, be adaptable to changing behaviors, attitudes and mindsets, be positive and be intentional.

Even if you do not have all of these, if you have God and a trusted faith partner, you can do whatever you set your mind to doing. I hope you allow my journey, experiences and lessons to encourage you on your faith journey.

Intro

Nothing flourishes unless someone or something has been nurturing it. Nothing. Not gardens, plants, pets, talent, skills, love, physical and mental health, careers, employees, business, etc. In order to flourish, you must do something. It must be watered. Allow me to use a vegetable garden as an example. When you first plant vegetable seeds you must be sure that the ground is prepared for what it is about to receive. So, you break the ground up. You till the ground to make it supple for planting. You choose the seeds and dig the hole where it will begin its new life. You cover it gently; patting it firmly and deep enough in the ground so that animals and birds won't steal the precious seeds you've just planted. You may even surround the planter or area with fencing to keep these animals out. You are protective of this seed because you know what you want to harvest once it has grown. You also protect it because you know how much work you put into beginning this process. You take care to maintain the garden by plucking up weeds that could possibly strangle your sprouts as they begin to spring forth from the ground. You water the garden, especially during those hot months where rain isn't as plentiful. You nurture it by fertilizing the ground. I've seen where people nurture their gardens and plants with loving words. At times it may look like they aren't growing. What you're waiting for isn't happening. It just takes time. It takes work. You can't just begin a process and walk away thinking that whatever you want to see is just going to sprout out on its own overnight. Not at all. You must do something in the meantime. If you neglect your garden, your crops will die, you won't have a harvest and you just might go hungry and become malnourished. No one wants that, so you must water those seeds, talk to those plants and encourage them to grow. Plant lovers know exactly what I'm talking about.

But here's the thing. When you plant a garden or begin learning a talent or whatever, you don't see the rewards right away. You have to wait. You have to practice, read and study. When you are anticipating, you must be sure to be patient. Nothing grows overnight. There's a process. It's the same way for you and I. When we are looking to have something major in our lives, just thinking and wishing and praying isn't always enough. Sometimes, a lot of the time, it takes work.

What kind of work and what does it look like? It looks like inner work. It looks like changing behaviors, patterns and processes and consistent actions that lead to the end result. Sometimes that takes making mistakes. It is from the mistakes that you learn. Making a mistake should not discourage you, but rather encourage you to keep going. The mere fact that you made a mistake speaks to the fact that you are actively pursuing something. It requires learning from others. Most importantly, it requires leaning in and trusting God. Yep, trusting God.

Isn't it funny how we can trust another flawed individual, program or process before we trust a perfect God? I mean really. The track record for humans is riddled with failures. And, yes, we get back up and keep trying. What would happen if we all trusted God from the beginning? I'm not saying our lives would be perfect, but we would certainly have less failures, less heartaches, less disappointments, less disasters, and less divorces. Proverbs 3:5-6 (NLT) says it like this: "Trust in the LORD with all your heart; do not depend on your own understanding. Seek His will in all you do, and he will show you which path to take." If we look to do His will rather than our own, I'm sure the outcome would far exceed our expectations. When we trust God with our seeds from the beginning, He sends people to water them and He increases the harvest, the outcome. What would it look like if we trust Him fully from the beginning every time?

Life to the Full

John 10:9-11(NKJV)

"I am the door. If anyone enters by Me, he will be saved, and will go in and out and find pasture. The thief does not come except to steal, and to kill, and to destroy. I have come that they may have life, and that they may have *it* more abundantly. I am the good shepherd. The good shepherd gives His life for the sheep."

If you know my story, then you know that I was in a short, but abusive marriage. I ignored many of the signs in the beginning and early in the relationship. I wanted what I wanted because I was 37, never married and no children. So, rather than wait on God, I took matters into my own hands and met, married and had a child within 11 months of meeting my now ex-husband. During the marriage, there were indications that I was not living the life of abundance. It wasn't a healthy marriage. I just knew that if we continued on the path we were on, one of us would end up in jail and my daughter would be without a parent. I didn't want that parent to be me. I was not happy and in fact, I became quiet, heavy inside and was beginning to be depressed. This is the total opposite of who I am. December 2014, while sitting on the side of my bed, I was looking out of the window. My thoughts went to, 'this can't be the life that Jesus died for me to have. This is not an abundant life.' It was at that moment that I made a choice. I wanted life to be more fulfilling for myself and my daughter. More importantly, I wanted to live.

I do not take it lightly that I survived because truthfully, it really could have gone a different way for me as well. I'm thankful that it didn't. On my drives to and from work I was able to have time to think and seek God, and decided that I wanted more for my life and my daughter. I think it is important to say here that even though I decided I wanted more; I didn't immediately act on it. I was uncertain of what that looked like and the path to take to get there. So instead of jumping out there, I went to therapy. I can remember sitting in my therapist's office. She gave me a note card and asked me to write my top 3 goals that I wanted to accomplish within the next 5 years. I can remember writing 1. Fix my credit. 2. Increase my credit score. 3. Buy a house for my daughter and myself. I was planting seeds and didn't know it.

A few months later, I left my abuser and moved in with my parents. It really did feel like a step backwards. Several steps actually. It didn't look like I was flourishing abundantly at all. For a while I had the mindset that I would be a statistic. That I would never have more and never be in a better position than sharing a room and a bed with my daughter at my parents' house. I took on depression and had a scarcity mindset. I only saw what I lacked and lived as though I had less than I actually did. I felt like I would never have enough to do the things I wanted to do. But I smiled every time I walked out of my door. Sure, people saw the facade but not what was underneath. When I got tired of feeling low, having anxiety, PTSD and depression, I went right back to therapy. It was with her help that I made some life changes and began to see that I could have more. At that time, all I wanted was more peace in my thoughts. When you're going through different transitions in your life, it's easy for negativity to take over. But I had to fight. I had to pray and believe that peace and a better life were available to me. I needed peace in my mind so that I could think clearly and be present for my daughter who wasn't even 2 years old at the time. I needed to be able to quiet the voice of the enemy who was trying to kill my future. Peace came when I started believing that God had more planned for my life.

I started working on my credit and with consistent action, got rid of debt. I made efforts and did ok, but the game changer was when I finally filed bankruptcy. Oh, I know that doesn't sound like flourishing. It looked more like another step backwards. Let me tell you why. Many in my life were not taught that bankruptcy could be a vehicle for starting over. Business owners use this method all the time as an opportunity to restructure and rebrand themselves. It gives them a fresh start. When I got past the thought in my head that I was regressing, it was a game changer. So, I filed bankruptcy and got rid of all of my bills, except my car loan. I went back to living on a budget. Paid off my car loan and within 2 years, my credit was repaired. #1 and #2 on my note card had been accomplished. Not because I did so much, but I decided in my mind that I wanted it and believed that it was available to me and reached out for assistance. It took time but I did it. It took faith to press through and get it done. The outcome was different than I expected but it led to a greater reward.

It didn't stop there though. My confidence level still needed much work. I was still at my parents' house, sharing a room with my growing daughter who had every doll and plushy created. It was time to move in year 3 of use living with them. However, my confidence had taken such a beating, that I talked myself out of it several times. I even had anxiety at the thought of moving. It baffled me because I bought my first condo at 25 then sold that condo and used that money to open a boutique and salon. How was it so hard for me to believe that I was now capable of taking care of myself and my daughter on my own. The negative self-talk

I had and the pressure I placed on myself about my ability to do it was unprecedented. But I knew it was time, and I still didn't move. I found places, began the application process, but was discouraged to continue because I had a bankruptcy on my record. Some of the applications actually said that if you have filed bankruptcy within the last two years then you can exit the application now. I was hurt because I wanted to rent that house for me and my daughter. Another reason I chose to stop. In year 5 when I was taking my daughter to her good Chrisitan private school (something I believed God to be able to do), she suggested I take a short cut. What did she know about a short cut at the age of 6? Anyway, I turned and saw some apartments. She said that they were really nice and we should live there. I put in my application and this time, I prayed and believed God for a second chance. This time the application asked if I had filed for bankruptcy. I hesitantly selected YES. In the past, the application process stopped there. This time, they asked why. For the first time, I was able to explain why. I did and I asked God to make it so if it is His will. A day later, the apartment manager called me and said they reviewed my application and read my story and said, "we believe you deserve a second chance" and offered the apartment to me. I cried the big ugly cry, right there at work. You have to believe that it is possible and act. You have to listen to the small voice with a message just for you. It can come from any place, even a 6-year-old child. You must understand that even a setback can work for you.

Before we move on, I want to share this with you. Another desire of mine is to be in a place where I can take care of my parents. In my mind, I wanted to have so much money to do all the things I envisioned in my head. Keep that thought in mind because I'm going somewhere with it. My daughter and I lived in our two-bedroom apartment for a year and a half before I bought my first townhome. Yep, I was able to purchase my parents' home which made it easier for them to build their dream home. They left equity in the home for me and I freed up money for them. #3 on my note card had been accomplished and I was thankful to be able to be a part of my parents' dream coming true. It took 6 years for me to accomplish those three goals. Mostly because I lacked confidence and moved slowly. But I did it. That little bit of faith that I had was all I needed and look at how God used all of what I went through to bless my life.

According to the National Coalition Against Domestic Violence, 1 in 4 women and 1 in 9 men experience severe intimate partner physical violence and 72% of all murder-suicides involve an intimate partner; 94% of the victims of these murder-suicides are female. I am compelled to caution you here. Domestic abuse is not only physical, but mental, emotional, financial, spiritual and verbal as well. Please take time to learn the various ways intimate partner violence can happen. If you find that you are experiencing any of them, please reach out to the National Domestic Violence Hotline at 800-799-7233. Abuse of any kind is not ok and it is not love.

Where it Started

In July 2023, a good friend asked me to be a part of the Ignite Empowerment Summit. I eagerly said 'YES'. She gave us free reign to speak on whatever God gave us to share with the audience. So, I asked the audience "What would you do if you only had 15 Minutes?" because I literally had 15 minutes to speak. Whew! I can talk for more than an hour with ease. So, I asked, "Lord, what do I share in 15 Minutes?" He said to me, 'Share your story'. So here is the extended version of that 15 minutes.

Every year, God gives me a word as a theme for my life. One year it was *Clarity*. Then it was Immeasurable. Another year it was *Consistency*. Next it was *Be Intentional*. Another year it was *Focus*. Last year it was *Take Authority*. In 2024 and 2025 it is *Continued Focus*. Usually when I am preparing to do anything big or creative, I play a certain genre of music or a certain song. Other times it's a certain movie that I play in the background to inspire me. It's like I need a theme for whatever I'm doing to motivate me and remind me of my mission and who I am. It's something about words that moves me so much. They resonate in me and ignite a passion in me to dig deep. Do you have a phrase or theme?

So why do I get words rather than make a resolution? I am terrible with resolutions, but words that mean something to me, I got that. Did I mention that I wanted to be an English teacher when I was younger? I did, but I didn't go to school for that. However, I did have an opportunity to homeschool my daughter during the pandemic. That dream came true and I did teach English along with other subjects, but that's off topic. So, what's your theme song or word? I want you to write it down. You can think about what you want to be emotionally or physically, or where you want to be in life; free, secure, etc. If you don't have a word or phrase, you are welcome to borrow one of mine until you decide on one for yourself.

So why did I decide to share this story? Well, I felt that it was important for people to know that even after you're progressing in life, there is still more to do and develop in order to move to the next level. Life is always moving and if you have desires to live a certain way, it will take an elevated version of you to maintain that certain way of living.

In 2023, I had these dreams that really unsettled me. They were prophetic but I didn't get it. They were warnings, but I didn't understand them. I shared the dreams with the other person involved, but they didn't get it either. I knew they were warnings and I trusted that God would reveal the dreams to me. Fast forward to a year later, I felt like God arrested me and swept me up in a whirlwind. He took me on a journey of discovery that I didn't expect. You see, what I didn't share with the audience was that I was in a very private recovery from a relationship that abruptly ended at the very beginning of that year. What a way to start the new year, right? God totally arrested me in that relationship and began talking to me about my entire life. I cried. I cried A LOT! Let me explain more here. This was a situation that had progressed to the point where I just knew it would lead to marriage. When the new year came around, I thought that what I would hear was a marriage proposal. Not at all. What I heard was they had to go their own way. I heard nothing from God, but I prayed. I prayed prayers of faith that I would hear from God. That He would tell me what was happening. I just knew God had an answer for me. I was believing that He would tell me things would be okay and they would turn around. What I got from God was, "Let Go." I'm not talking about a whisper. It was a pulling away, an untethering that I felt in my belly the very moment God spoke to me. There was no way of denying that it was Him.

During the process of healing, getting over and letting go, I wanted to hold on because I wanted to believe that all of the promises made should be, would be kept. I looked to man to keep a promise of protecting and providing for me, when honestly, I should have been looking to my Heavenly Father for that. To say it was hard to let go is an understatement. And what was I holding onto anyway? A promise that wouldn't be fulfilled, dreams that had to die, and unrealistic expectations that had to be quieted. Why was I holding on? Because I thought I needed something tangible to anchor me. I needed something or someone tangible here. I was afraid of what it would feel like to be completely alone. Not lonely, just alone. I was afraid to let go because I would have to face what I had been denying all along. That this wasn't going to be what I wanted; I couldn't make it be that; I couldn't do enough; and I couldn't say enough; I couldn't be enough. It was ending and I was scared of being alone. Who was going to take care of me and my child? God told me, "I got you. I'm taking care of you. I always have and I always will."

I needed several confirmations from people who didn't even know what was going on to tell me to Let Go. I did it but it was a process. Proverbs 3:5-6 (NKJV) "Trust in the Lord with all your heart, And lean not on your own understanding; In all your ways acknowledge Him, And He shall direct your paths." I had to lean on much prayer and fasting to move forward when I really wanted to stay where I was comfortable. Comfortable in the space where neither of us was thriving, but staying because of the time invested. Let me tell you really quick what staying somewhere too long will do to you. It will make you miss out on opportunities presented to you. You put your dreams and desires on hold or you slow walk them. You put everyone else's needs, dreams and desires ahead of your own. You help them get started, do the work and excel. You focus your energy on everything else except what you have been designed to do. You neglect other responsibilities. You get stagnant and sometimes quit altogether. It gets really easy to abort mission after mission for the sake of comfortability. It can lead to resentment and an unfulfilled life. There is nothing flourishing about that. But when you trust that God's got you, you can do anything. Even the hard, seemingly impossible things. Philippians 4:13 (NKJV) "I can do all things through Christ who strengthens me." I needed His strength to let go.

Another thing I had to do was forgive. Whew! That forgiveness journey is no joke because you want to stay mad and bitter. But what good does it do? When God told me to forgive and pray for this person, I thought it had to be cruel and unusual punishment. Here I am sad and heartbroken, and God is telling me to pray. What did I do? I prayed and forgave. It was the best choice ever because it allowed the letting go process to be so much easier once I finally accepted that it was for my good. Plus, I knew there were things I needed forgiveness for and I wanted to be obedient. Matthew 6:15 But if you do not forgive men their trespasses, neither will your Father forgive your trespasses. When God tells you to forgive, you must. After I forgave and let go, I can't describe to you the feeling of weightlessness I felt. It was like boulders were removed from my shoulders and cinder blocks removed from my feet. I finally felt like I could move from the space I had been in for many months. I felt light again. I felt like I could start getting back to me and the things God had given me to do.

After I let go, it was like God said, FINALLY! What He showed me on this journey was that although He gave me these amazing ideas and visions and purpose, the only reason they had not fully materialized was because I had placed so many other things in front of Him. I had other things I deemed more important. Exodus 20:5 (NKJV) states, "You shall not bow down to them or worship them; for I, the Lord your God, am a jealous God…" I was guilty of that. There I was again, asking for forgiveness. Do you know that this is something we must always do? It should become a practice and part of your prayer each and every time you pray and before you ask for anything; forgive and ask for forgiveness.

The other reason some things had not happened was because I did not have enough faith. I was looking to other people to validate me and my ideas. I kept enrolling in courses because I thought if I got more training then somehow that would translate into me being successful. NOT. I had to do something with what I learned. Then, I was looking for people to give me permission to do what I was told by asking if they thought it was a good idea, running details past them, and asking their opinions about an entire program that God had already given me. How could someone else's opinion be greater than God's? It didn't stop there. Because if I wasn't doing all those things, I was bringing them along for the ride. Trying to fit them into the plan so that I wouldn't have to go alone. It wasn't for them though. That's not all. For years I was living a life waiting on others to give me the crib notes and cheat sheets of what they did to be successful in business, in their finances, in their careers, and their relationships. What I came to realize is their life ain't my life. Their journey ain't my journey. This time with God showed me that I had to totally trust Him and what He told me to do. Jeremiah 29:11 (NKJV) "For I know the thoughts that I think toward you, says the Lord, thoughts of peace and not of evil, to give you a future and a hope." There is no way to flourish and live an abundant life if you're looking for people to validate what God has already promised and ordained. You'll miss out on the life He is providing for you.

So, let's go back to one of my theme phrases. "Take Authority." I searched scriptures to see what The Word said about authority. Luke 10:19 states, "Behold, I give you the authority to trample on serpents and scorpions, and over the power of the enemy, and nothing shall by any means hurt you." I had to see that I have authority to defeat anything that keeps me from doing what God gave me to do. Not even my own thoughts nor the opinions of others, or my self-defeating behaviors like procrastination and over-thinking. I have power and authority over all of it. I have authority to change my mind and my behaviors. He's given you that same authority.

Luke 19:17 (NKJV) states, "And he said to him, 'Well done, good servant; because you were faithful in a very little, have authority over ten cities.'" Here, I understand that the few things that God gave me to do with coaching, writing books, mentoring and helping others were all the seemingly little things. Now, I must take authority, stop thinking small when I know that God has matured me and elevated me to another level. Where He is taking me, I can't afford to misunderstand my position or misrepresent

Him in my work. I must operate with authority. He has given me everything I need to succeed. It's timeout for waiting for someone else to give me the green light. I give myself permission to sit at the table with other decision makers and make life better for others.

It's time for you to take authority.

Faith to Pray

Have you ever been in a place where you know you need to talk to God, but you're afraid to? I'm not talking about being afraid in a way where you have to be timid. I'm talking about the way where His track record in your life speaks for itself. Where you know if you go to Him, He just might answer, quickly. The fear comes because you may not be ready for the answer or resolution, so you hold out for a while longer, waiting for things to work themselves out.

Maybe you are afraid to pray because you really don't know if He will answer because it's been so long since you talked to Him. So, you just don't say anything at all, living in your discomfort and what-ifs.

Maybe you want to pray about a new situation and you just don't know how or if you should.

Maybe you've prayed and prayed before and still no answer, so you don't know if you should even continue to pray about the situation.

I'm here to tell you, I've been in each of these spaces at different times in my life. You see, God does not play when it comes to me. I know now that if I pray, then He will answer. It's either, Yes, No, or Wait. The challenge comes in having faith that prayer will work in your particular situation. Sometimes life can beat you up to a point where you just feel hopeless and you feel like nothing will turn around for you. You don't tell your friends or family because they can't help you. You don't attempt to talk to your parents because your relationship with them wasn't the greatest. They never listened, so how can you trust a God you don't talk to or share your most intimate thoughts with. Then there are times when you haven't spoken to God in a long time. Maybe you strayed away from your beliefs, your church or your circle of believers. Let me tell you what this does. It leaves room for more detachment and distance between you and God. It leaves room for the enemy of our thoughts to creep in and make you condemn and shame yourself. You feel like you don't deserve to talk to The Father. My friend, that is not up to you to decide. God is always there waiting to hear from us.

He longs to have a conversation with you. He longs to be in a relationship with you. There is so much He has in store for you, but you've got to be courageous enough to go to Him in prayer. What is prayer and what does it look like? Luke 11:5-13 (NKJV) says it best, "**5** And he said unto her, Which of you shall have a friend, and shall go unto him at midnight, and say unto him, Friend, lend me three loaves;

6 For a friend of mine in his journey is come to me, and I have nothing to set before him?

7 And he from within shall answer and say, Trouble me not: the door is now shut, and my children are with me in bed; I cannot rise and give thee.

8 I say unto you, Though he will not rise and give him, because he is his friend, yet because of his importunity he will rise and give him as many as he needeth.

9 And I say unto you, Ask, and it shall be given you; seek, and ye shall find; knock, and it shall be opened unto you.

10 For every one that asketh receiveth; and he that seeketh findeth; and to him that knocketh it shall be opened.

11 If a son shall ask bread of any of you that is a father, will he give him a stone? or if he ask a fish, will he for a fish give him a serpent?

12 Or if he shall ask an egg, will he offer him a scorpion?

13 If ye then, being evil, know how to give good gifts unto your children: how much more shall your heavenly Father give the Holy Spirit to them that ask him?

If a friend will give you what you need, then why wouldn't your Heavenly Father? You only need the boldness of knowing who you are in Him and who you belong to.

Let me share a little about where I was and how I approached prayer then versus how I approach prayer now. In the years before having my daughter, I did everything on my own. Everything I needed and wanted; I worked for it. If I had the money to buy what I wanted, I got it. I bought my first home by myself. Sold that home and renovated a building to open a boutique and hair salon. Closed the salon and started rebuilding my life. When I bought groceries, most of the time I brought them in my home by myself; all 10 bags at once because I didn't want to make multiple trips. I fixed things in my house and often assembled furniture by myself. I was used to doing things in my own strength. Even when I got behind on bills or needed extra funds, I didn't go to God. I worked a second job and saved and made arrangements. In my mind, there was no need to go to God about something that I could take care of myself.

After a while, life got real. There were situations I couldn't handle on my own and because I didn't have a strong prayer life, that wasn't my immediate go-to. I had not really talked to Him or needed Him in this way before.

Then, life got out of hand and out of desperation, I went back to what I knew, my last resort, prayer. One thing I learned was that I couldn't be timid. When you are desperate for God to answer and show up, you cannot be afraid. But here's the thing. Even though I was desperate, I still wasn't vulnerable, open and completely honest. I only took what I thought He could or should handle and I kept everything else to myself. I didn't totally trust and depend on Him to answer everything. Just the things I didn't have answers to, like my relationships. I kept that conversation to myself because if I talked to Him about them, then I had to confess my faults too. I was not doing that. But God is so kind and merciful that He met me where I was. He answered where I was. This built up my trust in Him. This helped me to know that I could trust Him even more to handle me and all of my issues.

Little by little, my faith grew. Not just in God, but in my prayers. I started having more faith to pray because I knew God was going to answer. Whether it was YES, NO, WAIT, MAYBE, NOT NOW. I had faith in our conversation and relationship. I had faith that He would hear me and my heart. I now have faith to pray about everything concerning me because I know He cares about all the things concerning me. Our relationship is beyond reciprocal. I pray, He answers. I talk; He talks back to me. I trust, He leads. I bring my needs, He provides. I bring my praise and worship; He envelops me with even more love.

Having faith to pray is simply believing that He wants to hear you and cares about everything concerning you. He's waiting to hear from you.

Faith in Prayer

Now why did I separate faith in prayer? Because it's so much deeper than just talking. Yes, I'm jumping right in. Faith to pray requires you to have faith to talk to God. Faith in prayer is believing that while you're praying God is moving. It is believing that whatever you are praying for, God already has it and it is being released in your life. It's like this. There are blessings with your name on them stored up in heaven waiting to be activated by your faith. Faith that it belongs to you. Faith that you can have whatever it is you need and desire in your life. Sometimes it's deliverance, other times it's freedom, and then there's strategy on the next steps in your life.

While growing in faith, faith in my prayers was essential. This happens when you practice praying God's Word back to him. Why do I say practice? Because we don't come into this world knowing His Word, how to pray, nor how to believe in prayer. Just like we don't come into this world knowing how to play sports or talk or play instruments. We must practice in order to get better at it. We must read His word in order to know what His promises are, what His corrections are, what He desires for us, and His plan for our lives.

So, here's what I did. When I was growing, and I'm still growing, I asked God to show me that He hears me in some small way. I asked Him to show me in a way that only He and I would understand and know. Sometimes it was a certain word that I needed to hear. A random person to confirm that I was on the right track. And do you know what He did? He answered in a way that I could understand. By the random person and the specific word. As I've grown in faith, He's answered during the prayer through words, phrases, scriptures, visions and sometimes dreams. The key is to believe and stay connected to Him, believing in Him.

After a while, I started believing in my prayers and thanking Him during my prayer time for the very thing I was praying for. I began having faith that what I needed, He already provided, even though I haven't received it yet. What I prayed for, would show up, even if it wasn't tomorrow. I began looking with eager anticipation of the day it would arrive on my doorstep or in my life.

Let me tell you about a young man's family and how they prayed for him. He and his sister had grown up in the same household. Went to the same church most of their lives. Then life started happening. He decided that he no longer wanted to be in a relationship with his mother and sister who were the two that always had his back. He decided to cut them off. Well, the mother was hurt. Can you imagine, the son you gave birth to decides that he no longer wants to talk to you and ignores your messages and calls? The sister was devastated by it. She was hurt because her mother was hurt. She was hurt because her brother was hurting and he wouldn't or couldn't even explain why.

So, the sister started praying for God to intervene. For God to soften her brother's heart (Ezekiel 36:26 -NKJV). For reconciliation between the mother and son. She started thanking God in advance because she had faith that God was hearing her prayers and He was working things out. One of his sister's prayers was that God would speak to his heart. That He would bless him and protect him wherever he was. She believed that God was working on him and she praised God during her prayer time for delivering.

After about 9 months, the son received a call from his grandmother, a devout woman of God, who knew what was going on. She told him to work things out with his mother. The son listened. He called his mother. They reconciled and now their relationship has been restored. The sister believed and God answered through her grandmother. She could have easily been discouraged, but because she practiced praying and practiced believing AND because God kept showing up, she knew He would again, no matter how long it took. Practice believing and thanking while you're praying and waiting.

Not only should you practice praying, you also have to have a certain posture while in prayer. A posture of praise and thanksgiving (Philippians 4:6 & Jeremiah 30:18-20 - NKJV) are also essential. It is my opinion that when we go to God in prayer, before asking for anything, it's a good thing to sing praises, worship and thank Him for who He is and what He's already done. Your posture of prayer should be one of humility like a child; open and available. For instance, the summer before my daughter began 6th grade, we decided we would go back to homeschooling when my daughter came to me and said, "Mommy, can I talk to you for a minute?" I saw the look on her face. It was pensive. I could tell she had practiced what she wanted to say and was building her confidence to say what she needed to say and to make her points. She began by asking me if we could possibly try public school since we were in a new county. She then gave me three reasons why she thought public school would be a good option for her. Then reminded me of my words that we could try it in a new county. When she was done talking, I said to her, "Well, it seems like you've thought about this and since I did say we could try it, I'll keep my word. Let's do it." She was shocked and happy that I said yes. She was humble in her approach and confident in our relationship that she could ask me whatever she wanted to ask and I would answer her. When a child is seeking something from their parents, they humble themselves and are available for their response. They are confident in their position and humble in their approach. Humble because they respect and revere their parents and confident because their parents can and will deliver. There's a difference. Will and Can. They believe both about their natural fathers and mothers. Why is it so hard for us to believe this about our spiritual Father?

Not only must we be humble, but we should also have a mindset rooted in who God is and what He is able to do. When you pray, believe that He is able, that He can, that He loves, that He delivers, that He has all power. Whatever you believe God is able to do, go into prayer knowing in your heart and beyond a shadow of doubt, that He Is. Have faith in who He is. Ask yourself, "What do I believe God is able to do?

If you're praying for deliverance of a loved one, believe that He is a deliverer and that they are delivered, while you're praying.

If you're praying for an increase in your finances, believe He supplies all of your needs and the increase and that it's on the way while you're praying.

If you're praying for a better life, believe that Jesus died for your better life and it's happening at that very moment.

If you're praying for a new home, believe that God can and He is sending you the right people at the right time in the right neighborhood, with the right neighbors at the right price and the right interest rates.

It may get challenging because we want things to happen in our own time. Sometimes things and situations look like they are just too far gone or too hard, but there is nothing too hard for God. There is nothing He cannot handle. When you believe and have faith while you're praying, you are believing and having faith in God. Keep having faith in Him. He will not fail you.

Faith to Endure - Trust the Process

Before we dive in, I'd like to share with you some definitions I found while researching the word Endure.

Endure: remain in existence; last; to remain firm under suffering or misfortune without yielding

Synonyms: face, experience, put up with, live through, brave, abide, persist, survive.

As I ponder these definitions, they all remind me of the strength that one must have in order to endure. I think of countless situations where we've all had to endure something.

You know, when God makes you a promise, it doesn't always show up right away. Sometimes there's some growth and development that needs to take place. Other times, events need to happen to prepare the way for your promise. This reminds me of when a woman conceives, she knows she has the promise of a baby, **prayerfully**. Her body goes through all of these changes. There is much discomfort as her body shifts, grows and makes way for the growing promise. Her hands and feet swell, her senses are heightened, and she wants all types of food to feed and nourish herself and her growing baby. She must endure all that she is experiencing in order to get to the end. Oh, but let's not stop there. Some women, like myself, experience long hours of labor. 23.5 hours to be exact. During those 23.5 hours of labor, I couldn't quit, I couldn't give up, I couldn't say, 'never mind'. I had to remain firm under the suffering of labor pains. Why? Because I knew the promise was a healthy baby girl that I had prayed for. The one that I petitioned God for. The one I sang to, read to, and talked to before she even arrived. The one I had prepared my life for.

How many times have you prayed for something and then given up because it was either taking too long, or it was 'too hard', or you had to give something up or acquire something new, or work with new or difficult people, or whatever your thing was? I'm telling you, sometimes that waiting period felt like torture. Like you would physically die if it took any longer. I know I'm not the only one who felt that way. But something inside of you wouldn't let you die. Something inside of you wanted to see what the end result would be because you had a promise.

No matter what definition resonates with you, know that it takes faith. When things in life get difficult, I pray that you do not quit. The one thing I regret is the many times in my life that I aborted missions because I didn't have the faith to persist when things got difficult or when things took too long or when it wasn't going the way I thought it should. I did this a lot in my younger years. I often wonder what my life and some of those ventures would have looked like today. I sometimes wonder how successful those plans would have been had I persevered with faith. What if I had had faith to face the insecurities that plagued me? What if I had faced these things head on and pushed forward? What if I had just held on to the little faith that I did have. The faith and excitement that I had when I began the journey in the first place. What if I had just endured the growing pains that came with maturing and healing? Maybe that's just it. Maybe we run from the thing that we need the most because of the discomfort and unfamiliarity of it all. Maybe we run because we believe that we have to have "big faith" for everything. Matthew 17:20-21(NKJV) states, "So Jesus said to her, "Because of your unbelief; for assuredly, I say to you, if you have faith as a mustard seed, you will say to this mountain, 'Move from here to there,' and it will move; and nothing will be impossible for you." When you activate and operate with mustard seed faith, you can endure, you can persist, you can live through, and remain firm.

When I was preparing to write this chapter, I was watching some TEDx Talks of some strong women. They encouraged me to be authentic and persevere. I really needed to hear something encouraging because I honestly didn't know what or how I would write this chapter and make it make sense. It has taken me over two months to write anything other than the chapter title. But I wasn't going to give up on this. Anyway, one of the women said the word 'dare' in her speech. Something in me lit up. I immediately came up with this acronym to use for anyone who is battling with her faith in her enduring season.

D - Decide that you're going to survive. You must declare this for yourself. Make it your mantra. I will survive this. Even with God's correction, I will not die. Psalm 118:17,18 (KJV) I *shall not die, but live, and declare the works of the* Lord. *The* Lord *hath chastened me sore: but he hath not given me over unto death.*

A - Acknowledge that God is always with you in the face of any enemy or challenge. He will not leave you nor forsake you. God is sovereign. Acknowledge that you have faith. Mustard seed faith is faith. Deuteronomy 31:6 (NKJV) *Be strong and courageous. Do not fear or be in dread of her, for it is the Lord your God who goes with you. He will not leave you or forsake you.*

R - Redirect your thoughts, Remain firm and Reliant on Christ. When you find that the gremlins are taking over your thoughts, redirect them to positivity and most of all, to the promise of what God has shown you and told you. Stand firm in your conviction that there is nothing that you and God together can't conquer. Rely on Christ to give you strength and perseverance. Philippians 4:13 (NKJV) *I can do all things through Christ who strengthens me.*

E - Execute before you change your mind and before fear slides in. Execute knowing that God is establishing your steps and thoughts and plans. Don't delay. Psalms 37:23 (NKJV) *The steps of a good man are [d]ordered by the LORD, And He delights in his way.*

You see, when you're waiting for things to change or happen in your life, it may come with some difficulties and maybe even sacrifices. This happens because change is uncomfortable. This happens because a shift needs to happen so that you're ready for what's to come. It is important not to quit and not to give up. Remember, you are stronger than you think. When we are weak, God is always strong. We can draw strength from Him. As my good friend Jalissa Spence stated, "Ask God to build our endurance."

My friend, abide in Christ while you're waiting. Be brave and have faith in God that He will see you through, He will strengthen you, He will plant you on firm foundation and He will sustain you as you remain in Him.

Faith to Speak It

I used to think that the only people who could "speak a word over" someone's life were prophets. Ha! I know better now. But really, when you are not informed and not taught, this is a belief you carry. Not knowing that we have power and authority to speak life into our own lives. You may have heard this scripture, Proverbs 18:21(KJV) "Death and life are in the power of the tongue: and they that love it shall eat the fruit thereof." How about this one, Mark 11:23 (NKJV), "For verily I say unto you, That whosoever shall say unto this mountain, Be thou removed, and be thou cast into the sea; and shall not doubt in his heart, but shall believe that those things which he saith shall come to pass; he shall have whatsoever he saith."

It's one thing to hear it all of your life, but if you have no understanding of how it applies to your life then they are just scriptures you memorize and recite because they sound good. Good old 'Christianese'. At some point, you have to start understanding and believing what you have read and what you have said.

It has been my dream for quite some time to own a single family, detached home of my own. I have always loved looking at houses and dreaming of what it would feel like to live in one of these magnificent homes. Well, the time came and went for me to buy a house. I heard it prophesied over my life that I would buy a home. I've had dreams about it countless times, but still didn't move. My feet were stuck. I felt like the houses I liked were unattainable. So, I didn't pursue them. I started looking at houses that I thought were in my visual range for my salary and status. Single mom, single income, single credit, single budget. Well, one day God told me that I will buy a new house and it will be just as I see it in my mind. I know what I see and the area. Another time, I was told it would be in the area and school district I desired. I began asking people to pray for this to happen. I really needed to ask them to pray that God would help my unbelief, but I'll get back to that in a minute.

The problem wasn't so much that it was not attainable. It was that I didn't believe the promise of Ephesians 3:20 (NKJV), that God would do exceedingly, abundantly, above all I could ask or think, just for me. I believed it for others, even prayed for others to get what they wanted in a home, a business, or whatever situation. However, I didn't have the language or courage to speak it over my own life. If my words have power, then why didn't I use that same power for myself? When I finally decided that I was going to move forward, I had a dream about a specific realtor friend. In the dream we were out all day looking at homes. When we returned to the house I was living in at the time, a sign was in the window that it had been sold. In my dream, the house had literally been sold while we were out looking for my next house. I had no choice except to find something because I would literally have nowhere to live. I took it as a sign to move forward. I called the realtor and we began the process. I stalled for a minute until my realtor said to me, "we need to sign this listing agreement." It was seemingly out of the blue, but it really wasn't.

Next, I was supposed to visit a friend, but we canceled and I went to a coffee shop instead. This is where the last confirmation happened. For about a year, a gentleman had been sitting in the coffee shop every time I went. He was always on the phone and on his laptop. This particular day, I decided that when he got off the phone, I was going to ask him what he does all the time in there. God is clever because I didn't think that I would do it, until I recognized that he had a Bible on the table next to his laptop. Bingo! We've got something in common. So, I asked him, 'What do you do in here all the time?' He said, "I'm a life coach." I almost fell out of my seat. When I told him I am a life coach, we kept the conversation going knowing that we had that in common. I asked him what area he focuses on. He went right into telling me he leads with his Bible, with the Word. Here's where it got interesting. He began telling me his testimony. Wouldn't you know it? It was about how he thought a house that still needed to be completed, that was sitting on a hill with a gully behind it was actually his house, but he thought it was unattainable. He would go to his spiritual leaders and tell her what he needed her to pray for. She simply said, "Let it be so." Finally, she told him that he didn't need to keep coming to her, he simply needed to go to his Father. He did and began speaking over his own situation. Long story short, he bought that house, believing God every step of the way. He bought the unattainable house by saying, "Let it be so." He spoke it and he believed it and so can you.

So how does this apply to me and you? I continued going to the coffee shop here and there. We had great conversations. One day he did an illustration using my laptop. He opened it. He said that on one side of the laptop screen is everything I am believing in God for. The only thing in the way is doubt. He closed the laptop and said that once I let go of doubt, all of it would be available to me. I believed. Fast forward to 2024. I sold the townhouse and bought a single-family home, with land all around, a four-car driveway, near the beach, in a neighborhood I desired, with wonderful neighbors and a school district that cares for the children. It was as I saw it and God delivered.

Faith in Letting Go vs Faith to Let Go

There are times in our lives where God requires us to let go in order to move forward. Let me tell you this, letting go can be really easy for some people and some situations. But for others like me who are dedicated and loyal, we find it hard to let go because we feel like we are giving up. I am not a fast quitter. Sometimes it's the familiarity of it all. Sometimes it is the comfort of it all. Other times, I'm trying to prove a point to myself: I won't prematurely abort the mission.

When God has instructed you to let go of something, it's best you do it the first time He says it. This is what it can sometimes sound like. First it may be a thought in your mind. That's easy to brush off and dismiss as a random thought. Next it may come as a message in a sermon or a show or podcast you're listening to and something inside of you resonates or becomes a bit unsettled at the thought of letting go. After that, you may have a dream or vision that you just can't shake. If you're anything like me, it takes all of that and then some more. The 'more' looks like this. While you're praying about it, God tells you audibly to let go along with a feeling of a tug in your belly like something pulling away. That scared me, shook me and grieved me all at the same time. And, I was in awe because I had not heard God speak to me like that. Literally audibly and physically. It blew my mind. You would think I would have let go, but I didn't. It took two more people to tell me to let go. One person just said it while he was talking to a group of us and just called me out. The other person said she saw in the spirit that I was in a tug of war with God. Now, if I was in a battle of tug of war with God, who do you think would win? I decided at that moment, with tears rolling down my face, that I had to have faith in letting go knowing that God already said He would take care of me and would fulfill all of His promises.

Having faith in letting go is like knowing that if you release something or someone from your life, it will make room for what God wants to deliver to your doorstep. The letting go is the breaking and the rebuilding all at the same time. It's the release and recovery at the same time. It's forgiving and healing at the same time. You've got to have faith in the process of letting go. It isn't always easy. Faith in the process is trusting God to guide you when you don't know where you're going or where you'll end up. Take a breath right here because I know it may have triggered someone. Having faith in letting go is you having faith in God that your future is secured.

Now faith to let go is what I struggled with because I really didn't know if I could do it. I had held on to this person and these habits for so long that they were a part of me. So, God was asking me to let go so He could do something different. So, He could tear up, break up and dismantle some things then establish me with a new and more solid foundation. I thought I wasn't ready because all I knew was all I knew, and for real, I was okay with that. But God wasn't. He wasn't okay with me living beneath my birthright. If I'm His daughter, then I need to live like that. I needed to act like it. AND there are rewards and benefits I need to experience because I'm His child.

For weeks I fought this letting go. After remembering that vision of the tug of war, I gave Him a yes and finally let go. You see, for months I had been fasting, praying, dreaming and journaling. When I let go, I went back to all I had declared and decreed over my life. I went back and read all of the promises revealed during prayer. I read all of the anchor and reference scriptures and memory verses that I'd written in my journal. I read all of it during my prayer to God and I said, Lord, I'm letting go because You said You would take care of me so I'm trusting You to keep Your word. I took a deep breath and let go. Each day after that, when I found myself wanting to pick that thing up again, reach back for a person to steady me, or find comfort in a human, I asked God to help me let go again. I did it every day until I no longer had that struggle.

I had to have faith to let go. Faith in what God said and what He had shown me. Let me tell you this, when I let go, that's when opportunities came. That's when connections started. That's when I got my smile back and I felt lighter. The faith to let go, comes from your certainty in Who God Is and all that He is able to do. Even if you don't know what the next step looks like, having faith in Him who is the light in the darkness is all you need each step of the way. From the day I let go to today, He has been providing me with everything I need. Just like He promised.

Lack of Faith vs Faith-Challenged

You know, when I would hear someone say the reason something hasn't happened was because someone lacked faith. In some cases, I believe that may be true. Lack of faith, to me, means that you have no faith at all. You may say to yourself, "But I'm a believer, I should have faith." My challenging question is this; what is it called when you have faith, whatever you're waiting for hasn't happened, you believe it can, but you're not quite sure it will. Maybe because of past history with people. Maybe because it's always taken a long time or it didn't happen the way you thought it would. Instead of lacking faith, maybe some of us are faith-challenged. We have it, but the challenge comes in consistently activating our faith. Or when our faith is challenged, we cower away because it's simply too hard. The thing we want 'costs too much'. It's taking more faith than we really want to exercise. When I was looking up the definition of challenged, I found the words that explicitly describe what I felt and wanted to say.

To challenge or be challenged means several things but I will list just a few here.

To dispute especially as being unjust, invalid, or outmoded: IMPUGN - to assail by words or arguments: oppose or attack as false or lacking integrity

To confront or defy boldly: DARE -: to challenge to perform an action especially as a proof of courage

To order to halt and prove identity

A calling to account or into question: <u>PROTEST</u> - the act of objecting or a gesture of disapproval

The act or process of provoking or testing physiological activity by exposure to a specific substance

To demand proof that something is right or legal

An objection to something as not being true, genuine, correct, or proper or to a person (as a juror) as not being qualified or approved

A request to disqualify a trier of fact

After reading some of the definitions, which one of those rings true for you? I'll share that mine was that I always wanted proof. What did that look like? I wanted to know the end and all of the details in between. I wanted to know a fulfillment date. The date that God was going to deliver what He promised or what I requested. I believed that He could do whatever He said, but my problem was believing that He would. I was faith-challenged.

What do you do if you have been faith-challenged?

Well, first we must know what has been hindering your faith from flourishing.

Limiting beliefs. I didn't know my full potential. Or maybe I did and was too afraid of how big it really is. Can you relate to any of this? If this is you, I'm going to share with you what helped me and you are free to borrow some or all, but most importantly, you are encouraged to follow the path God has for you.

Read, Study and Remember the Word. In His Word are promises. When you have studied His Word, you can use it to encourage yourself. His Word serves as a reminder on those hard days.

When you study, His Word builds you up and strengthens you so that you can fight the negativity and doubt that tries to creep in.

Remember the prophecies you received. One of the most poignant things that pushed me through a home selling and buying process was to remember prophecies and visions spoken to me and over me. I wrote them down and recorded them so that I could review them. In my prayer time, I reminded God of the words spoken to me through His servants and the dreams and visions He'd given me. Surely, they won't fall to the cold, hard ground. They were good seeds that were planted and needed to be watered. I told the Lord I believed His Word and I believed His servants and I believed He wants me to have everything that was spoken. So, I remind myself and keep forging on.

Take your eyes off of other people's blessings and timelines. Sometimes paying more attention to what someone else has received after they fasted and prayed one time, you feel like it's supposed to happen the same way for you. But what if that person had been fasting, praying, sowing, serving and sacrificing for years? What if that person kept aborting the mission and finally got in alignment and God finally released the blessing. The thing is, if we focus on God and build our relationship with Him, we will see that the way He relates to us is unique and specific to us. Some of us, God has to be REAL patient with because we take our time. Some of us just have blind faith and whatever He says, we go with it. I'm working on becoming the latter.

Practice having faith. So, building this faith muscle isn't the easiest thing to do. We want things fast and now. Faith requires discipline, focus, dedication, patience and belief.

1. Take your eyes off of other people, because their lives ain't your business anyway. It breeds jealousy and envy. I know because I became envious of the blessings taking place in someone else's life and they were someone I loved. God quickly checked me and said, anything I do for them, I can do for you. My blessings don't run out.

2. Permit yourself to actively operate in the gift and purpose God planted in you. If you don't know what that is, I encourage you to seek God for your answers. Sometimes you just need to look at what you're passionate about and start there. Just like what was shared with me some time ago and it has always helped me get back on track. Go back to the last thing God told you to do. Sometimes it's the first thing. You'll find your answer there. And when you go back, remember the zeal and excitement you felt in that moment. Harness it and use it to encourage yourself again. This is how you give yourself permission to live.

3. Stop being timid! Remember you have power.

   a. Psalm 91:13 (NLT) You will trample upon lions and cobras; you will crush fierce lions and serpents under your feet!

   b. Luke 10:19 (NKJV) Behold, I have given you authority to tread on serpents and scorpions, and over all the power of the enemy, and nothing shall hurt you.

4. Know who and what the enemy of your faith is?

   a. Limited thoughts

   b. Limited beliefs

c. Self-sabotaging behaviors and patterns

d. Negativity spoken over your life

e. Memories that haunt you

f. Residue of a relationship that was bad or ended badly

g. Jealousy

h. Envy

i. Insecurity

j. Abandonment

k. Daddy Issues

You identify your own enemy, put it under your foot and apply pressure to it. You have the power and authority to tread on all of these and crush them under your feet and it shall not hurt you.

Here's what you do now? Commit yourself to actively operating from a posture of faith, belief in God. Remind yourself of who He is and believe that He will come through for you. If you are faith-challenged, then exercise your faith even more to build that muscle. You can do this by trusting God in the small things. He is concerned about those too. Go back and remember His track record. Take note of His receipts. There is perfection in all He does. When you remember all of the ways God has delivered and made good on His promises, then it makes trusting Him with more and the unknown that much easier.

Pray with Your Whole Heart

Mark 11:24 (NKJV) Therefore I say to you, whatever things you ask when you pray, believe that you receive *them,* and you will have *them.*

So let me park right here for a minute since we are talking about having faith to ask for what we want. Sometimes that asking comes in different forms. A declaration, a decree, a car ride conversation with God, or a designated time in prayer. 1 John 5:15 (KJV) "And if we know that He hears us, whatever we ask, we know that we have the petitions that we have asked of Him." But let me first tell you what I did to hinder the release of the blessing I was praying for. I prayed half-hearted prayers. I prayed but I didn't really believe what I was praying for was available to me. Because I had been disappointed in the past, I just felt like it wasn't for me. You see, man will let you down. But not God. And I had to learn to not see God through the same lenses. I had to learn to see Him in a different way; as a Father. I'll talk more about that later. It wasn't for me in the way I thought or the way it was given to someone else.

We give our all to everything else; scrolling social media, meal prepping, extra-curricular activities. However, when it comes to prayer, we see it as a chore and want to do a quick drive-by prayer but expect immediate results and complete fulfillment of the blessing.

One day in prayer, God said to me, "No more weak prayers". I guess it was time to go deeper. I couldn't believe He spoke to me like that. But like a good father, He had to be real and honest with me. He had to give me a hard truth. A wake-up call. So, I asked

"Lord, what does that look like?" He said, "pray bold prayers." Ouch! Bold prayers?! That would mean I had to be honest, open, exposed and trusting. I didn't want to be exposed. I didn't want to pray the bold prayers because that meant another level of faith would be activated. I asked and He answered, so I had better do something with that information. I couldn't unhear it. So, I started getting bold. It was scary at first. But God is so merciful. He met me right where I was. I felt like the Holy Spirit was encouraging me each time I came to Him. In my prayer time, I learned that I couldn't just run through a prayer like I was reciting the alphabet. I learned that I could go to God and spend time with Him. Asking Him to increase my faith. Help my unbelief. Increase me in knowledge, wisdom and understanding. Help me to see myself like He does. Show me His way. Show me how to trust. Open my eyes and ears so that I could hear Him more clearly and see more in the spirit rather than with my natural eye. This doesn't happen overnight, but with earnest prayer and intentional focus, it can develop. I know because it has and is happening for me.

So, when you pray, really believe that you are going to receive the desires of your heart. God can answer and then He supersizes it. You just have to believe that He can and He will. Go to your Father and present your big issues and pray big bold prayers. "To know the love of Christ which passes knowledge; that you may be filled with all the fullness of God. Now to Him who is able to do exceedingly abundantly above all that we ask or think, according to the power that works in us, to Him *be* glory in the church by Christ Jesus to all generations, forever and ever. Amen." - Ephesians 3:19-21(NKJV).

Remember to Whom You Belong

Deuteronomy 14:2 (NKJV) "For you *are* a holy people to the Lord your God, and the Lord has chosen you to be a people for Himself, a special treasure above all the peoples who *are* on the face of the earth."

John 1:11-12 (NKJV) "Even in his own land and among his own people, the Jews, he was not accepted. Only a few would welcome and receive him. But to all who received him, he gave the right to become children of God. All they needed to do was to trust him to save them." If we are children of God, then that has to mean that He is our Father. I like to call Him A Good Good Father.

When you hear the word 'father', for some it can bring not so pleasant memories and feelings. Let's be real, there are some fathers and mothers who are not present in their children's lives for whatever reason. Some are not present physically, emotionally, financially, nor spiritually. They're just not there. Then there are those who are present, but their presence fills the home with hurt, anxiety and pain. Then still there are those who don't know who their father is. There's a woman I know who can attest to what it is like to have a dad who was physically in the house, on a part-time basis, but not emotionally connected because of his own issues, secrets and addictions. Can you imagine what it's like to find out at 12 that your dad isn't your father and that someone else is. That person couldn't be in her life for his and her mother's own good reasons. You see, people make the best decisions they can with whatever information, knowledge and understanding they have at that time for all parties involved. Because of the decisions of her parents, she felt the effects of abandonment from both situations, and neither were intentional. They just could not be avoided. Not that her parents meant to hurt her, but because it simply couldn't be helped. So, because of unfavorable circumstances like this one, we look at fathers through a distorted lens. We see them the way our predicaments presented them to us. We see every man the way we see or saw our fathers. I'm here to tell you that it isn't fair. We must seek to learn the real meaning of fatherhood so that we can experience it in a more real and loving way. The way God intended for it to be.

Psalm 27:9-10 (NKJV) "Oh, do not hide yourself when I am trying to find you. Do not angrily reject your servant. You have been my help in all my trials before; don't leave me now. Don't forsake me, O God of my salvation. For if my father and mother should abandon me, you would welcome and comfort me." Deuteronomy 31:6 - "Be strong and courageous. Do not fear or be in dread of them, for it is the Lord your God who goes with you. He will not leave you or forsake you." This is a promise from Him. Because we know God's track record is perfect and we know that He will never leave us, we can trust that He will always be there, and that He will always keep His Word, just like a good father would.

[1]A father's presence in a child's life matters. It is essential. According to an article in Focus on the Family, "A father's gifts of quality time, life-giving words and positive actions have a long-lasting impact on his children." It is paramount to the development of their character, identity, mental, emotional, spiritual, and

---

[1] https://www.google.com/url?q=https://www.focusonthefamily.com/parenting/fathers-matter-the-importance-of-a-father/&sa=D&source=docs&ust=1736225198707784&usg=AOvVaw2kWGqGFSd3RvLwLiPsPhEe

physical stability. His presence provides strength (Philippians 4:13), inspiration, encouragement, confidence (1 John 5:14), comfort (Psalm 23:4), productivity (Proverbs 6), and a strong foundation (Luke 6:47-49). These are just some of the qualities that Our Father provides for us, and He gives all of these freely. We do not have to perform, we do not have to beg and plead. We simply receive them because we are His children. Period.

Likewise, there is nothing a good father will keep from his children (John 14:13-14). There is nothing that a good father won't provide for his children (Matthew 6:26 & Philippians 4:19). There is no love like a father's love (John 3:16). He makes provisions for you (2 Corinthians 9:8). He protects you (Isaiah 54:17). He cares for you (1 Peter 5:7). He gives you peace (John 16:33). He pursues you when you lose your way (Matthew 18:12-14). He permits you to come back to Him (Luke 15:11-32). You are His child and He will guide you (Isaiah 30:21).

When you forget who you are and what God has promised you, think back to what His Word says to you about you and who you are to Him. I believe that because we are joint heirs with Jesus, we are also God's beloved sons and daughters. Remember that He cares for you and there is nothing Our Father won't do for us, if it is in His will for our lives.

Remember, you belong to The Father who created everything. He knows you inside and out because He created you. So go back and find your identity in Him. Not in people, not in material things, not in status or titles or positions. Only in God can we find our identity. Once you do, hold on to it and never allow anyone to tell you anything other than what God has shown you and told you. You are God's child. Believe that and believe Him for all that you need.

Big God, Big Ask

Proverbs 3:5-6 "Trust in the Lᴏʀᴅ with all your heart, And lean not on your own understanding; In all your ways acknowledge Him, And He shall [a]direct your paths."

When we are talking to God, it's easy to ask for the everyday essentials. "God bless momma, daddy, sister, brother, children, spouse, home, friends, food and things we need to survive. But what about when the thing you desire in life or the purpose in your heart requires more than a blessing for loved ones or over your house? What if the thing you need to flourish in this life is so big, it's kind of scary? So, you don't ask because you've never known anyone to ask for it and it feels weird. Or, because it would require something from you that you aren't sure you can handle, but you knew you want it. You know, one of the reasons I was not flourishing like I thought I should be because I was wanting more but too afraid to do the work to get it because I knew it would cost me and challenge me to level up. It would require a different version of me. Some things required inner work. What He showed me required Faith work. I didn't have the confidence; therefore, I wasn't even asking Big Enough. In all actuality, I was doubtful that I could do the big things He gave me to do. One thing I learned is that doubt will defeat you before you ever get started. Sometimes, I have to remind myself that God chose me and gave me a vision and had a plan for my life before I was ever created. The plan He had for me required me to do big things. John 15:16 "You did not choose Me, but I chose you and appointed you that you should go and bear fruit, and *that* your fruit should remain, that whatever you ask the Father in My name He may give you." If this has already been the promise from a Big God, then what's the problem with asking for Big Things?

Here's what that looked like for me. It was Spring 2020, I wanted to hear from God because I felt big things were going to happen. Have you ever felt that? Like you were on the verge of something spectacular? A good friend sponsored me for a bootcamp that I wanted to attend. It was for aspiring life coaches. After the bootcamp, I enrolled in the certification and mentorship course. During that same time, another friend gifted me and my daughter with a one week stay at her timeshare in Williamsburg, VA. I knew that I wanted to use that time wisely. So, before I packed up my daughter and myself and set out on my way to Williamsburg, I asked God to speak to me. I was still participating in the daily classes, taking notes and praying. After class one day, I went into the bedroom and sat in the middle of my bed, papers, pens, highlighters and my Bible all over the bed. I sat there and asked God what I was supposed to do. Where am I supposed to coach? That may not seem big to you, but it was big to me because I was starting something new. I was walking into seemingly, unchartered water. I said, whatever You tell me and whoever I coach, God, please let it be impactful for them and profitable for me. Let it be life changing. Yep. I was not going in timidly. He spoke to me and told me exactly who to call. It was as if He was sitting beside me. I wrote down the name and the organization and made the call when I returned home. That one call led to me coaching three groups of women, three days a week for 6 months, with a 5-figure profit. I went from zero clients and zero money to over 30 women overnight and enough money to assist people in my life. But it didn't stop there. My biggest ask is to have a resource center for women survivors of domestic abuse. A place where she can receive not only tangible resources needed to launch her new life of freedom, but intellectual, emotional and supportive resources that she can use to change the trajectory of her life and the lives of her children. I just believe we can break the cycle of domestic abuse one family at a time. The best part is the housing that my organization will provide that keeps in mind the integrity and economics of each family. That's my big ask and I believe it will happen. Because of this ask, people started donating items to me that were specifically for women transitioning from a shelter to their own homes. I raised money for a Laundry Detergent drive, so the women at the shelter would not have to choose between clean clothes and lunch for their children. I was able to help a couple furnish their new apartment after experiencing the devastation of being unhoused. Other mothers were able to get clothes for their teen daughters. And the best part to date, was being able to raise funds to help a single mother of five children get clothes, shoes, a year's worth of school supplies, Thanksgiving dinner and Christmas gifts for her family. This was definitely impactful and moved me to tears on many occasions, because God showed up and showed out in a big way each and every time.

Now, even though I have shared my vision for the resource center with you here, what reminds me of what I prayed and asked God for is a picture that my daughter drew of the resource center. Yes, even my daughter is aware of her mother's big dream and she is supportive of it, even at 11 years old. I also routinely read what I wrote in my journal. I write my thoughts and revelations on anything and everything around me. Sticky notes, bill envelops, receipts in my purse, journals, notebooks, and notes section in my phone. A friend gifted me a beautiful blue journal. I call it my Big

God, Big Ask journal. In it I write all of the big things I'm believing in God for. Things that I can't articulate to people because I don't want to be discouraged anymore and I don't want their opinions or criticism about something ginormous that God didn't give them to do. I don't want to hear that it can't be done or it's already been done. Sharing too soon can lead to discouragement if it's shared with the wrong people. (Choose your people wisely.) So, I write my big dreams and goals in this journal. Then I read it to God after I write it. I ask Him if it is His will. I ask Him to help me to see it like He sees it. Sometimes, it's so big and I ask Him why He gives those visions to me. I'll tell you. Sometimes we think we don't deserve certain things because we think we have to perform in order to receive them. We think we have to achieve a certain level of success or have a certain thing in order to be worthy of a big idea from God. Nope. According to 1 John 3:22 "And whatever we ask we receive from Him, because we keep His commandments and do those things that are pleasing in His sight." We've got to have faith in what He promised and believe that it is available to us too. We've got to have faith to believe that the big, abundant things are for us too. So don't be afraid to ask for big and the capacity to manage it well.

Ask God to ignite something in you that will never go out. Permit yourself to stay lit for your purpose and your life.

From this day forward, you are a flame that represents God and everything that represents Him is illuminated, it is good and shall prosper.

Friend, it's timeout for living in fear, lack, with a scarcity mindset, as low hanging fruit, depleted, inconsistent, accepting less than we deserve, and unfulfilled. It's time out for living a mediocre life when we were meant to experience abundance in every area of our lives. Whatever it is that you've been sitting on, it's time to ask God to ignite it again. It's time for you to take authority and live big.

Here's what I want you to take from this book. In order to flourish, you must have faith. You must be willingly patient. You must trust. You must choose. You must be persistent in your pursuit.

Last story before you go. During one of my numerous conversations with my mother, I asked her what she thought was the difference between faith, trust and belief. We talked for a while. My mom shared with me what she had been talking to the Lord about that morning. It sounded like she had gone back into prayer again. It got me excited! I was responding and agreeing. Here's the thing that struck me. She said, "Ronni, I don't think I have a challenge with believing and trusting and having faith. I have all of that. I also have concerns. She explained that with everything she has seen and has experienced, she's trusted God to take good care of her and knows that He's got her and my dad, but that still doesn't stop her from having concerns. Notice she said concerns and not worries. There's a huge difference. You know what that did for me? It set me free because it perfectly articulated what I had been feeling. I had been so hard on myself about this faith journey. I even asked God, "what more must I do to show that I have faith in You? Tell me what I need to do." While my mom was talking, I was crying because I felt something breaking off of me. And do you know what it was? Self-condemnation. I heard God say to me while my mother was talking, "stop condemning yourself." I had been condemning myself because I thought my faith and the results of my faith were supposed to look a certain way and because it didn't, I thought I wasn't doing it (faith, trusting and believing) right. I cried some more.

So, friend, you may be in those same shoes. I want you to know that whatever faith you have, you're doing it right and it's enough. Build on it, grow in it, stand in it. Whatever you do, you must not waiver, and you must keep going. Remember, there are better days ahead of you, so use your faith to push you to it.

My prayer for you

Dear God,

The woman reading this book right now picked it up because she has a desire to learn more about faith. More importantly, Lord, she desires a deeper connection and relationship with you. God, I know that you are a loving Father and that you have had our lives planned since the beginning of time. Thank you, Father, for being so intentional about our lives. You don't treat any of us the same, yet all of us feel special. Lord, show my friend who she is in You, who You designed her to be and the purpose for her life in this world.

Lord, I pray that her faith increases daily and that she will see that her faith doesn't have to look like anyone else's. That her crazy faith in You will not have her to be ashamed. Your word tells us in Psalm 37:18-19 'The Lord knows the days of the upright, And their inheritance shall be forever. They shall not be ashamed in the evil time, And in the days of famine they shall be satisfied." Lord, help her to see that her future is secure in You.

Father, I pray that she continually seeks You and finds You everywhere. Help her to know that you are always present and available. Abba, hear her cry and answer in ways that leave no room for doubt. Even in the seemingly little things, You still show up. Thank You, God, that she can give all of her worries and concerns to you.

Jesus, even when things seem out of control, assure her that when she relinquishes control to You, life works out so much better. Walk with her as she continues to surrender her will for Yours.

Let her desires become what you desire for her and that as she gives you her plans, you order her steps to accomplish them.

God, whether my sister is new on this faith journey or she wants a closer relationship with you, help her to know that even though faith can look like a free fall or a trust fall, You are always there to catch her in Your loving arms. In Your arms is such a beautiful place to be. In Your arms, there's security, there's freedom, there's hope and peace.

Last, Father, help her to know that her mustard seed faith is enough. She doesn't have to live up to anyone else's standard of faith. I pray that she knows that her faith is enough, her belief is enough even if she has concerns, because we are human. Help her to not condemn herself for not living up to a standard that the world has sat before her. Free her of self-condemnation so that she may have liberty, humility and boldness to come to You for help, no matter what.

God, thank You for choosing her. I pray that she remembers Your promises and Your perfect track record on delivering her. Bless her in every area of her life and that she enjoys the life you are providing for her. Change her, renew her, transform her and establish her according to Your will.

Lord, I love You and thank You for being a Big and Faithful God. In Jesus' Name I pray, Amen.

www.ingramcontent.com/pod-product-compliance
Lightning Source LLC
Chambersburg PA
CBHW061718120626
46550CB00003B/1271